WEIRD BUT TRUE SCIENCE

Weird But True Human Body Facts

Series Science Consultant:
Mary Poulson, PhD
Central Washington University
Ellensburg, WA

Series Literacy Consultant:
Allan A. De Fina, PhD
Dean, College of Education/Professor of Literacy Education
New Jersey City University
Past President of the New Jersey Reading Association

Carmen Bredeson

CONTENTS

digest (dy JEST)—To change food into smaller parts that can be used by the body.

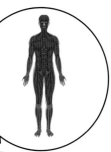

muscle (MUH sihl)—A part of the body that helps us move.

oxygen (AHK sih jen)—Part of the gas we breathe. We need oxygen to live.

Our Human Body

Did you know that you can't tickle yourself?
Or that your tongue is a **muscle**?
The human body is amazing!
All its systems work to make you what you are—
even if some of it is kind of weird.

Let's read about some weird—but true—body facts!

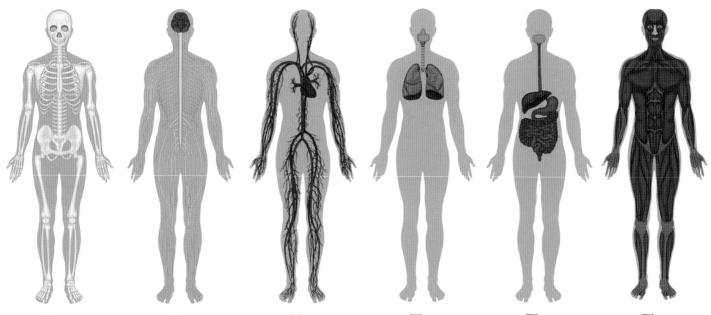

The
skeletal
system is full
of bones.

The
nervous
system helps
you feel, think,
taste, smell,
and more!

The
circulatory
system uses
the heart
and blood.

The
respiratory
system is for
breathing.

The
digestive
system
helps you
use food.

The
muscular
system lets
you move!

LAUGHS

THE MORE THE MERRIER

A great big laugh is good for the body. It makes the heart beat faster, just like running does. It also brings extra **oxygen** into the body. Your body needs this gas to live. Best of all, laughing makes us feel good. It even makes sick people get better faster! HA, HA!

It's weird, but it's true!

Skin

What's in that Dust?

New skin cells grow all of the time.
What happens to the old skin? It falls off.
As many as 50,000 tiny bits fall each MINUTE!
Most of the dust in your house is really just little
pieces of dead skin.

It's weird, but it's true!

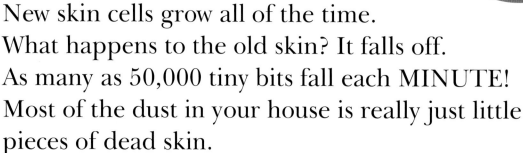

These flakes of dead skin are shown
more than thirty times their real size. ▷

TONGUE
WHAT A MUSCLE!

Did you know that your tongue is a very strong muscle? It moves in all directions. A tongue helps you say words. It helps you swallow food. Each tongue has its own print pattern, too, just like your fingerprints.

It's weird, but it's true!

SNEEZE

Get out of the way!

Why do we sneeze? To get something out of our nose. It might be dust, germs, or even cold air. A sneeze sends air rushing out at up to 100 miles per hour. That is as fast as a race car goes. ACHOOOOO!

It's weird, but it's true!

Saliva

It's more than just spit!

Saliva is also known as spit. You make a lot of it each day—four to six CUPS! Without saliva, it would be hard to swallow. Saliva helps us taste our food and start to **digest** it. When you smell food, you start to make more saliva. SLURP.

It's weird, but it's true!

TICKLES

GIGGLE, GIGGLE

Have you ever tried to tickle yourself?
Try right now. Bet you can't do it.

Tickling works because you are surprised.
You can't tickle yourself because your brain
knows what is coming.

It's weird, but it's true!

Eye Mites

This mite is shown at about 800 times its real size.

You can't see them!

Tiny little bugs live on your eyelashes!
About half the people in the world have them.
Why can't you see them? They are too small!
They live at the bottom of the hair. They eat
dead skin and oil.

It's weird, but it's true!

Bones

Tiny Bones, Big Job

Half of a person's bones are in the feet and hands. NO WAY! Yes, they are. Each hand has 27 bones and each foot has 26 bones. That's 106 bones out of a total number of 206 in the WHOLE body.

It's weird, but it's true!

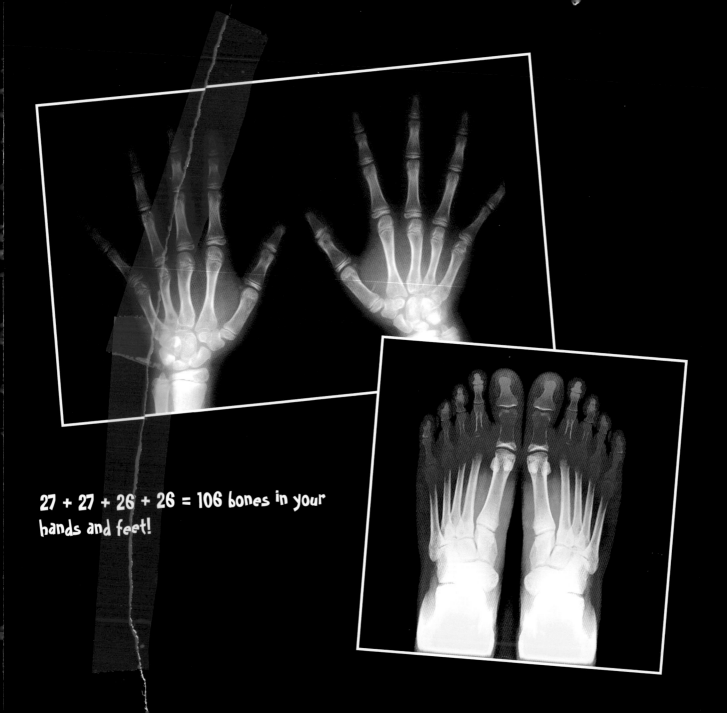

27 + 27 + 26 + 26 = 106 bones in your hands and feet!

LEARN MORE

Books

Kenah, Katherine. *The Bizarre Body*. Columbus, Ohio: School Specialty Children's Publishing, 2005.

Levine, Shar, and Leslie Johnstone. *The Amazing Human Body*. New York: Sterling Publishing, 2006.

Walker, Richard. *Eyewitness Human Body*. New York: DK Publishing, 2009.

LEARN MORE

Web Sites

Kids' Health

http://kidshealth.org/kid

Yucky Gross & Cool Body

http://yucky.discovery.com/flash/body/pg000029.html

INDEX

To our wonderful grandchildren: Andrew, Charlie, Kate, and Caroline

Enslow Elementary an imprint of Enslow Publishers, Inc.
Enslow Elementary® is a registered trademark of Enslow Publishers, Inc.

Copyright © 2012 by Carmen Bredeson

Library of Congress Cataloging-in-Publication Data

Bredeson, Carmen.
 Weird but true human body facts / Carmen Bredeson.
   p. cm. — (Weird but true science)
 Includes bibliographical references and index.
 Summary: "Discover why we laugh and sneeze, what dust really is, and why we can't tickle ourselves"—Provided by publisher.
 ISBN 978-0-7660-3865-3
 1. Human body—Miscellanea—Juvenile literature. 2. Human physiology—Miscellanea—Juvenile literature. I. Title.
 QP37.B8284 2011
 612—dc22
            2010035861

Paperback ISBN: 978-1-59845-369-0

Printed in China

052011 Leo Paper Group, Heshan City, Guangdong, China

10 9 8 7 6 5 4 3 2 1

To Our Readers: We have done our best to make sure all Internet Addresses in this book were active and appropriate when we went to press. However, the author and the publisher have no control over and assume no liability for the material available on those Internet sites or on other Web sites they may link to. Any comments or suggestions can be sent by e-mail to comments@enslow.com or to the address on the back cover.

Photo Credits: © iStockphoto.com/Jill Chen, p. 11; Photo Researchers, Inc.: © Eye of Science, p. 19, © Grapes – Michaud, p. 13, © Living Art Enterprises, p. 21 (feet), © Steve Gschmeissner, p. 9; © Photos.com, pp. 1, 6, 10; Shutterstock.com, pp. 2, 3, 5, 8, 12, 14, 17, 18, 21 (hands).

Cover Photo: © Photos.com

Note to Parents and Teachers: The *Weird But True Science* series supports the National Science Education Standards for K–4 science. The Words to Know section introduces subject-specific vocabulary words, including pronunciation and definitions. Early readers may need help with these new words.

Enslow Elementary
an imprint of
Enslow Publishers, Inc.
40 Industrial Road
Box 398
Berkeley Heights, NJ 07922
USA
http://www.enslow.com

3 9957 00168 5656